VEGETABLE GARDEN
FOR THE FIRST TIME

THE PRACTICAL & SIMPLE GUIDE FOR BEGINNERS TO GROW & COOKVEGETABLES

Fast & Simple Guide

Table of Contents

INTRODUCTION.. 6

CHAPTER 1 THE VEGETABLE GARDEN PLANNING.................... 12

CHAPTER 2 HOW TO MAKE YOUR BEST VEGETABLE GARDEN ON THE FIRST TRY 16

CHAPTER 3 BUILDING YOUR VEGETABLE GARDEN 24

CHAPTER 4 PLANTING YOUR VEGETABLE FOR SEASON 28

CHAPTER 5 MAINTAINING YOUR VEGETABLE GARDEN 42

CHAPTER 6 GARDEN PROCESS 52

CHAPTER 7 TIPS AND TRICKS TO AVOID PARASITES 66

CHAPTER 8 AROMATIC HERBS FOR ALL YEAR**S**...................... 70

CHAPTER 9 ADVICE FOR GROWING PLANTS FRUIT 80

CHAPTER 10 PROBLEM SOLVING 86

CHAPTER 11 FAQ.. 94

CHAPTER 12 WHAT TO DO WHEN WINTER GROWS NEAR 104

CHAPTER 13 10 RECIPES READY IN 30 MINUTES WITH VEGETABLE 118

CHAPTER 14 OTHER THINGS TO CONSIDER IN VEGETABLE GARDENING 138

CONCLUSION.. 150

Introduction

Modern methods of farming are rapidly growing less tasty vegetables. For other reasons than taste and nutritional content, plants are cultivated, i.e., their ability to survive intact transport and yield the highest harvest possible. From the farmer's point of view, this harms your cooking. Of course, you can choose to buy organic vegetables in the grocery store instead of everyday items. Still, it's difficult to find, and typically much more expensive.

You have complete control of what appears on the dinner table by increasing your own. You know exactly how new they are, what pesticides have been used to cultivate them, and how exactly they are–if a vegetable has no appeal to the broad market today, the chances to find it in a supermarket are small.

Don't worry; if you don't have sizeable garden-vegetable gardening is as effective in containers and pots as in gardens. Planting in containers in many respects is safer if you expand to a small extent, because the cups can be moved around the garden or the courtyard according to the environment. If you encounter an unseasonable freeze, you can cover the crops before the damage occurs. Some vegetables can be grown in a tub, also more massive such as pumpkins and squash.

Another way to grow vegetables on an allowance or in a community garden if you have limited space. Allotments are small parcels of land that you rent to grow vegetables or plants. They are very common in the UK and Europe. Still, they can also be found all over the west, mostly funded by municipalities.

You might well think you don't know how to grow vegetables at home-at this point, this can be accurate, but you can learn. You will soon reap the rewards of your plot of plants.

It won't take much time to gather a lot of useful information about growing vegetables, and there's nothing better than experience to support you on the path to a perfect garden.

You will need to learn other things related to your situation to grow vegetables at home. For example, how much sun does your selected area get every day? What are the conditions of your soil? By purchasing a simple kit from your local garden center or nursery, you can quickly determine the terms of your property. You can choose the right fertilizer for your specific soil conditions once you learn this.

Everything tastes as good as the vegetables you grew at home! If you buy it from the local store, it won't be new, and it won't take long before it begins to lose its flavor. Compare this to the vegetable garden before you cook your dinner, pick your desired food, harvest, wash and prepare it, and serve it with your meal what's fresher than that.

You should be able to enjoy healthy vegetable crops from your home vegetable garden, and you could quickly stop buying veg throughout the year. With today's economic climate this is an excellent bonus-so you won't just eat healthier food, have better tastes of vegetables, but you can save money!

It is a comfortable yet insightful introduction to people who are entirely new to gardening and want to grow vegetables. It offers step-by-step guidance for beginners who direct the reader through the selection of an appropriate plantselection area. This also presents several practical and theoretical vegetable tips growth and highlights some of its advantages in terms of money-saving and enhanced relaxation.

Now you understand which plants you would like to grow. Have seeds to buy. There are many sites on the topic, from garden centers to news agencies. Typical vegetable seeds are pretty cheap, usually under two or three pounds. Nevertheless, the number of seeds in a packet varies considerably depending on the type of plant. One packet of carrot seeds, for example, can contain about 100 grains, while a pack of boot seeds can contain only about 20. Such difference is generally proportional to the germination rate, with significantly fewer carrot seeds germinating than bean seeds.

Once you have the seeds, the next step is to plant them. This is usually the working part of the process. Many seed packs will have simple seeding, maintenance, and harvesting instructions for the crop that you plan to produce. If you have no guidance, there is plenty of valuable information on the Internet, and your nearest bibliothèque is also an excellent resource. There are numerous types of vegetables, and the demands and difficulties associated with each of them could fill up many books, so the rest will concentrate on general growth tips, rather than discussing all of these.

The soil it cultivates is one of the most elements of a plant's performance in its fundamental climate. The identification of your soil type and the compatibility with your plants can make a real difference in its growth. Nevertheless, the introduction of some fertilizer from a garden center will alter its characteristics and make a significant difference in plants ' health. This issue coincides with feeding plants as they grow. It is essential to focus on the feed given to the plants you plan to eat, so what you put on the roses may not be so good if you eat! There are several different organic feeds for very healthy vegetable plants. An interesting experiment is to purchase some and test them on a few of the same plants to see the output differences.

Chapter 1
The Vegetable Garden Planning

B efore you focus on the ever important soil, watering, and planting of your garden you first must plan. When gardening, it is crucial to know the size of your garden, the hours of sun access, wind, and more. All of these factors will significantly affect what you can plant and how well your crops grow. Thankfully, with a little knowledge, you can plan the perfect garden.

Garden Size

If you live in an apartment then you only have one option for a garden, which is to practice container gardening. Thankfully, there are many options for container gardening and you would be surprised by the crop size you can yield.

If you live in the suburbs or city with an average-sized yard then you should find that your garden is easily accessible from your house. Even if your backyard is on the smaller side, you should be able to plant a decently large garden if you practice gardening by the foot. With this gardening method, you can maximize your gardening space and crop yield with a little extra planning.

Lastly, if you live on a large property you can have an extensive garden. You will likely be able to not only provide enough crop yields for your family, but even excess to sell at the local farmers' market or to gift to neighbors if you desire. However, if you do live on a larger property try not to place the garden too far away from your home or a place where you regularly walk past. You want to be able to easily view and examine the garden daily so that you know when it needs to be watered, weeded, or harvested.

Sun Exposure

Some plants need shade. Although, most crops require ample sun exposure. Unless you are planning on growing shade-hardy plants you need to ensure that the gardening location you choose received a minimum of six hours of full sunlight daily.

Wind Exposure

Heavy winds can significantly damage a garden by breaking the plants and carrying away the precious and nutritious topsoil of a garden bed. Therefore, try to find a gardening location that is not overly windy. If you are unable to avoid planting in a wind-resistant location or live in an area that gets high winds, then you may need to build a windbreak for your garden.

Find Your Hardiness Zone

When planting, it is best to choose plants native to your area. These plants are non-invasive species which are designed to grow well where you live. You can easily find these plants by looking up the United States Department of Agriculture's (USDA) local hardiness zone map. This map is organized by ten different numbered zones. Once you know the number for your zone you can easily find which plants grow well in your local area based off of temperatures and other factors.

Create a Garden Wish-List

After you know your hardiness zone, create a list of all the plants within your zone that you hope to grow. This includes vegetables, fruits, herbs, and flowers. Some plants are annuals (grow year after year) while others are perennials (die off at the end of each season). You may want to organize your list between these two categories so that you can more easily decide where to plant everything.

Create a Garden Map

Measure out the exact garden space you will be using and then create a to-scale map on graph paper. When creating this map, you want to create a layout of where you will plant everything, keeping in mind to arrange it in a symbiotic manner. While doing this, you will need to know exactly how much space each plant will require, which you can usually find in organic seed catalogs and seed packets.

Schedule Your Planting

The seed catalog you purchase from should have details on when your seeds should be sprouted and transplanted. This will be impacted by your local frost-free date. You must ensure that you plant after this date, otherwise, the seedlings will die.

Chapter 2
How to Make Your Best Vegetable Garden on the First Try

Strategy to Raised Bed Garden

R aised Garden Beds shall be a garden bed that is raised above the surrounding soil or ground on which it is built. These frames may be constructed of a variety of materials, boards, bricks, stones, or wood. A hanged garden bed can also be used as an elevated bed.

The height of a raised bed and the length of each length are calculated for the protection of the garden. The 4-foot dimension is because a person can touch from both sides the central point of the garden. One downside of a bed with a long length is that it helps you to walk around the garden bed for a specific activity that involves a complete bed width, such as seeding or weeding. An uplifting 4-foot-by-8-foot garden bed is typically considered a suitable size for most gardens, as well as for planting and 8-foot woods that are accessible at most wooden courtyards.

A significant advantage of breaking a long garden bed into a shorter segment is that the amount of usable edge decreases. There is a concept of permaculture which needs to be introduced or for you to get an insight into the "edge effect" and the interface between two media, the intersection where different environments meet. This interface between two different ecosystems provides a broader range of favorable environmental conditions to support both animal and plant life and therefore have a high production capacity.

Raised beds will also encourage you to plant crops closely together as you don't have to leave spacing for walks, which makes them more efficient per square foot than the typical row gardening cycle. The benefits of high-density crops are also that plants that grow closely together shade bare soil and reduce weed growth.

Another value of a raised bed garden is the potential to retain a healthier soil quality. Owing to the convenient access of a raised garden bed, the soil is not compacted by walking the conventional row gardening strategy. This makes raised bed planting an excellent option for a no-till garden. If the soil is kept maintained by organic matter, the natural life that occurs in the soil will function for you. The layout of the field in a raised garden bed will profit greatly and have a growing crop.

Raised bed planting provides a fascinating option and a range of benefits over regular planting. When you look carefully at people's gardens from late, you can note the raised bed gardens come in or take over. Gardening is usually an enjoyable and successful workout. Growing your food will offer advantages and keep you bored.

First of all, raised bed planting deals with enclosed gardens, an elevated garden is a garden within a frame that is normally a few inches to a few feet high. The frames can be made of iron, wood, or whatever you choose to use. This may at first seem a bit strange, but it has its advantages.

The first thing that should be noticed is that it is harder for disabled people and those in ill health to focus. Since the garden is as big as you want, no bending is required. These gardening can be enjoyed only by people who use wheelchairs or with reduced mobility. Not to mention, the nature of the plants and the food provided by these garden forms is much greater.

Because the dirt should not be on the ground in a raised garden because no one walks on, it is no more stable than field dirt. It is another advantage over the usual planting of raised beds. When soil is not compacted, plant roots can disperse more quickly, enabling the plant to grow and thrive higher than on the bottom. Therefore, raised bed gardens can surpass normal gardens.

Not like it's a competition or something, but it's really important to all of us who cultivate our food. You can grow whatever you want in these gardens; it shouldn't be just flowers. Fruits, vegetables, and much more that can thrive in field soil can also flourish in an up-grown greenhouse. You will see how this could be a fun activity or an opportunity to educate your youth about gardening.

Another thing to note is that elevated horticulture cannot be performed outdoors. You can have your garden indoors, as long as you have a lot of sun and access to water. This is nothing new; plenty of us now have our gardens indoors. It can make it easier to deal with people, particularly those who don't have to leave the house or rain outside.

In closing, elevated bedding is a fascinating alternative to growing methods of gardening. Raised bed gardens are harder to do and are ideal for those who are unsafe or up in age. They make fun one and talk plays, not to mention. You can grow your fruits and vegetables as in all gardens, but I would prevent growing maize in your home on a high waist counter. Except with a tall roof, it

Growing Your Vegetable

When you would like to grow crops for food, it is quite simple to say,"I will only plant this package of seeds" and scatter the seeds in a row. However, how can you know you will utilize this produce? Just how much can you consume and how much are you going to give away? Rainwater has a limited quantity of space and it drives the gardener to arrange the greenhouse for greatest generation of any type of edible harvest. Receiving the ideal fruit and vegetable production from the greenhouse requires preparation. For example, assume you've got space at the greenhouse to make berries in 3 containers.

You may sprinkle seed to the strands in spring and then await fruit to look eventually in late night. However, with great planning and reasonable utilization of your greenhouse, then you might be harvesting berries nicely in the wintertime. In reality, at a heated saltwater you can harvest just about any vegetable plant during the entire year. Nevertheless, this will entail maintaining the rainwater in the minimum temperature of 60--70°F (16--21°C) through the winter months and supplying supplemental lighting.

Few farmers locate this efficient cost of electricity and cash. For all, it's much better to fit the harvest roughly to its favored period of growth and make the most of this greenhouse to expand the seasons as opposed to replace them. Tropical fruit is not the same story. To be able to continue to keep apples, guavas, or passion fruit living throughout the wintertime, you'll have to keep a tropical or warm greenhouse with a nighttime temperature of 50°F (10°C). Use your heated saltwater to maintain tropical fruits living during winter and move them on a sunny deck or patio.

To optimize space in the greenhouse, then think about which herbs and vegetables it is possible to begin at a germination chamber, and then plants it is possible to begin from the greenhouse and then proceed into the primary garden. A sensible strategy starts with deciding that fruits and vegetables that you would like to consume and then deciding how much you really would like to increase. Choose varieties that develop fast or which are streamlined. And utilize the whole greenhouse area, filling the greenhouse beds, planting in containers and develop bags, and coaching plants to expand vertically when potential.

Growing Vegetables from the Greenhouse

Suppose you enjoy broccoli and begin it on your greenhouse. If you begin a whole package of seeds you can grow around 2 hundred heads of kale. I don't know about you, but I find that excessive quantity of broccoli. Begin with considering the number of fruits and vegetables your family members might consume in your dinner table. Let us assume a household of four meals a head of broccoli a week that is fifty-two minds of broccoli annually. But a broccoli harvest will grow all at one time and won't create from summer sunshine, and that means you may split your plantings into orbit and fall plants together with twenty-six heads in every single harvest. You may use five or four heads clean and freeze the remainder for later usage. An alternate is to develop five thoughts ten times every year to provide you knew broccoli throughout the year and remove the need for a freezer. You can do this using a greenhouse; however, it also requires careful preparation.

Chapter 3
Building Your Vegetable Garden

I f you're building a vegetable garden you should pick the sunniest part of your garden possible. For flower gardens you'll be able to take advantage of darker areas by planting shade loving plants but for productive vegetables, that produce good crops, sun is essential. If you're planting both types of garden then reserve the best, sunniest area for the vegetables and fruit.

High levels of sun have many advantages for edible plants. It helps to make strong, disease resistant and stocky plants with plenty of bulk to them. It will also help to produce a sweet flavor in some crops including onions, carrots, chillies and tomatoes. Salad plants and strawberries may appreciate some shade but it's easier to create shade than it is to get try to get rid of it.

Raised beds will not be necessary in every garden but they may be useful if you have very poor soil, such as sandy or chalk based soils. It can be easier in these cases to simply create a whole new set of soil conditions rather than attempt to improve the existing ground.

24

Designed for Life

There is good life and bad life in every garden; healthy crop-producing plants are the good part of the equation. The bad part includes snugs and snails. In modern architecture the principle of designing to stop crime is becoming popular and you can use the same principles in designing the layout of your vegetable plot. Snugs and snails are the main anti-social elements that you'll want to discourage. Ideally put a path around your plot, using slabs, or simply compacted earth, and if the plot is big enough also add one through the center or even two to form four planting areas. The external path keeps weeds, plants and long grass from overshadowing your vegetables but it also stops them from being used as a handy hide-out for nighttime raiders of the slimy variety.

The pathways also create open ground to cross for the slugs or snails, which makes it easier for you and the local bird life to patrol. If you embed the paths so that they are slightly lower than your beds for the vegetables you can also sprinkle organic slug pellets at the edges of the pathway, turning them into an easy to reach "appetizer" for your unwanted guests. This should put them off the main course for good.

Keeping your plot weed-free and also free from dead leafs will help to ensure there is no cover for the intruders to make use of during the day when you're around.

Weed Wars

The best of us miss the odd tuber or root and if you've overlooked quite a few lives can be a constant battle against perennial weeds. Simply cover the bare soil areas with cardboard or a layer of old newspaper and add compost over the top. This should be enough to stop the weeds from springing up in the spring while it also remains easy enough to dig through when it comes to planting.

Good Advice and Bad Advice

If you're creating your first garden there is plenty of advice out there. Some will come from friends and family, some from books, magazines and TV shows. If that isn't enough you can always go on-line; in the end you'll have lots of advice and much of it will be conflicting! Here are some basic, solid ground rules over what to ignore and what advice to take:

Crop rotation is fine if you have a major agricultural business but it's not that suitable for small scale gardening. Crop rotation works on large farms because the turnover time on crops is relatively slow; in small gardens it's much higher and so makes less difference. Simply try to not grow the same crop on the same part of the ground two years in a row.

Sowing your own seeds is considered the correct way to establish your garden but it takes some practice. Don't be ashamed to buy young plants in your first year (or even subsequent ones). Some seeds, like chilies, may need heat propagators to start them, so simply go with young plants to get a good first crop and learn as you go with seeds! When you do begin to learn the art of growing from seed don't ignore the advice on the seed packet. Sowing early will leave the plants exposed to the incorrect level of light and the wrong temperature. This creates a weak start in life and they'll never fully recover. Ideally, plant in the middle or towards the end of the recommended sowing window for best results.

Don't ignore the frequently heard advice to make your own compost. It takes little time, uses up waste in an environmentally friendly way and saves you a lot of money! It's also the most natural form of food for your plants and they will thrive on it.

Chapter 4
Planting Your Vegetable for Season

PLANNING THE SEASON CROP-BY-CROP

You can plan the growing season using the number of frost-free days in your region-that is the time between the last frost in spring and the first frost in autumn. Choose crops that will grow to maturity between the last frost in spring and the first frost in autumn. If you want to grow outside of the natural season plan to use season extending devices such as row covers, polyethylene/plastic hoop tunnels, and a cold frame. There will be several varieties to choose from after you decide which vegetables you want to grow; some varieties will be ready early in the season, some mid-season, and some later. Some vegetables are easily grown from seed sown directly in the garden; others are best started indoors where the temperature is controlled and later transplanted to the garden when outdoor temperatures are favorable.

Cool-season crops (do best when the temperature is about 55° to 70°F):

- Beets

- Broccoli

- Brussels sprouts

- Garlic

- Kale

- Kohlrabi

- Leeks

- Lettuce

- Mustard

- Onions

- Parsnips

- Peas

- Radishes

- Rutabaga

- Shallots

- Spinach

- Swiss chard

- Turnips

Warm-season crops (do best when the temperature is about 65° to 80°F):

- Beans, snap

- Beans, lima

- Beans, shell (dry)

- Corn

- Cucumber

- Eggplant

- Melons

- New Zealand spinach

- Okra

- Peppers

- Potatoes

- Pumpkins

- Squash, summer

- Squash, winter

- Sunflowers

- Sweet potatoes

- Tomatillos

- Tomatoes

- Watermelons

- Zucchini

Mid-Winter / January

Slow and No Growth Period: No plant growth will occur outdoors during the days when there is less than 10 hours of sunlight. This period occurs over several weeks during early, mid- and late winter depending upon where you live. Plants and seeds in the garden during this period will sit idle; plants will resume growth when there are more than 10 hours of sunlight during the day. During the no growth period, protect crops from freezing temperatures by covering them with straw or protecting them under a plastic hoop tunnel or cold frame. When hours of sunlight each day grow to more than 10 hours, plants will resume their growth towards maturity

Beginning with the warmest regions first, here is a seed starting and planting guide for mid-winter-January.

Note: it is safe to plant or do any of the tasks listed for regions cooler than yours.

USDA Zone 10: No frost regions

- Sow cool-season vegetable seeds in a cold frame or plastic tunnel.

- Start warm-season vegetable seeds indoors; start seeds of tomatoes, peppers, and eggplants indoors.

USDA Zone 9: Low frost regions

- Sow cool-season seeds indoors in pots and flats or outdoors by mid-month. Cool-season crops include beets, carrots, cabbage family members, lettuce, peas, and spinach. Expect slow growing while the days are still short.

USDA Zone 7-8: some freezing possible and frost likely

- Start seeds of cabbage, hardy lettuces, and onions indoors under bright lights. When plants are about 4 inches tall set them out in the garden under cloches or plastic milk jugs and harden them off.

Cool-Season Crops for Planting in Late Winter

Cabbage is easy to grow and can be eaten raw or cooked. Cabbage also stores well either in the root cellar or in the form of sauerkraut. There are many cabbage varieties to choose from—green or red, smooth leaved or ruffled-leaved savoy, round-head, cone-shaped, and flattened-head. And consider days to maturity—early season, mid-season, and late season; late maturing cabbage (more than 90 days) is the best choice for storing in a root cellar for winter use; early- and mid-season varieties are usually planted in spring for fresh use midsummer and autumn.

Broccoli, cauliflower, kohlrabi are good choice for planting in late winter or early spring for harvest before summer heat. There are 60-days-to-maturity-or-less varieties for each of these vegetables. All like to start and come to harvest in cool weather. Plant these in a cold frame or under a plastic hoop tunnel or start these crops indoors up to 10 weeks before the last frost then transplant them to the garden as early as 4 to 6 weeks before the last frost.

PLANTING ZONE-BY-ZONE: March / Early Spring

Beginning with the warmest regions first, here is a seed starting and planting guide for late-winter—March. It is safe to plant or do any of the tasks listed for regions cooler than yours.

USDA Zone 10: warm weather

- Transplant to the garden tomato, pepper, eggplant, and tomatillo seedlings.

- Direct seed warm-season crops: beans, corn, cucumbers, lettuce, melons, okra, pumpkin, summer spinach, squashes, sweet potatoes, and watermelon.

USDA Zone 9: frost possible:

- In frost-free regions, set out seedlings of cabbage, eggplant, melon, okra, pepper, pumpkin, squash, and tomato seedlings started indoors.

USDA Zone 8: frost possible:

- When the soil is dry and workable, plant asparagus crowns, onion sets, and early potatoes. Prepare planting holes adding a layer of aged compost.

USDA Zones 6 and 7: freezing temperatures likely early—frost likely late:

- Place cloches or plastic hoop tunnels in position to warm up the soil.

- Move broccoli, cabbage, and cauliflower seedlings to a cold frame to harden off.

USDA Zone 5: freezing temperatures likely:

- Put seed potatoes in a warm, bright windowsill to encourage them to sprout

MID-SUMMER PLANTING FOR AUTUMN HARVEST

Plant in mid- to late-summer for autumn harvest, plant cool-season crops for autumn (and winter) harvest, cool-season crops get a quick start from seed or seedling in warm summer soil and come to maturity in the cool autumn days. For autumn harvest, choose crop varieties with shorter days to harvest so they will be ready before the first freeze. Here is a list of autumn harvest vegetables:

- Arugula

- Asian greens

- Beets

- Broccoli

- Brussels sprouts

- Cabbage

- Carrots

- Cauliflower

- Celery

- Chinese cabbage

- Collards

- Corn salad (mâche)

- Endive

- Escarole

- Florence fennel

- Kale

- Leeks

- Lettuce

- Mustard

- Parsnips

- Peas

- Radicchio

- Radishes

- Rutabagas

- Spinach

- Turnips

EARLY AUTUMN PLANTING TIPS

Sow winter salad leaves now. Here are some vegetable leaves that are good in salads and stir-fries: beets, broccoli, carrot, cauliflower, kohlrabi, radish, and rutabaga. All of these are cool-season crops you can grow in a cold frame or plastic hoop tunnel this autumn and winter. Direct sow these crops in the garden or in a plastic hoop tunnel or cold frame now.

Plant Chinese cabbage. Time to sow Chinese cabbage, bok choy, mizuna, mibuna and other cool-season Asian vegetables; Chinese cabbage grows best when days are growing shorter and cooler. The same for bok choy, snow peas, mizuna, and mibuna, sow these crops under a plastic hoop tunnel or cold frame in cold-winter regions. In warm-winter regions and reverse season regions these leafy crops can be grown in the garden.

Spring cabbage planting time, plant spring cabbage in beds that have been amended with aged compost and manure, where winters are wet, plant spring cabbages on mounds or ridges 9 inches high, add a pinch of bone meal into each hole at transplanting.

MID-AUTUMN PLANTING TIPS

Grow greens indoors this winter. You can grow lettuce and other greens indoors under fluorescent lights this winter. Choose trays or containers about 3 to 4 inches deep. Sow seed and place under the lights. Keep the soil just moist by setting the containers in shallow trays so you can water from below as needed. Harvest cut-and-come-again.

Garlic autumn planting, plump garlic cloves produce plump bulbs. Skinny cloves produce skinny bulbs. Plant garlic in sun-soaked, compost-rich, well-drained soil; set cloves 3 inches deep—deeper to 4 inches in cold-winter regions, 4 to 6 inches apart, time garlic autumn planting so that plants have time to sprout before the first freeze. Sprouting indicates roots are established.

LATE AUTUMN PLANTING

Plant corn (also called lamb's lettuce and mâche) in autumn, corn salad is extremely cold tolerant. It can be planted in mid-autumn for overwintering under a plastic hoop tunnel or cold frame. It can also be left unprotected in all regions except perhaps where the snow cover is very deep. There are two types of corn salad—large-seeded and small-seeded; small-seeded varieties grow best in winter (grow large seeded varieties in spring and autumn); plants can be harvested through the winter. Make successive sowing every 10 days.

Autumn lettuce and spinach sowing for spring harvest. You can direct seed lettuce and spinach in mid- to late autumn. If you want to harvest leafy greens through the winter grow them in a cold frame or under a plastic hoop tunnel. Sow seed so that there are six or seven leaves when the first heavy frost arrives. Before the leaves freeze, cover the plants with a thick layer of straw or chopped leaves or a portable plastic hoop tunnel. In early spring, pull the mulch back and cover the planting bed with a plastic hoop tunnel; the overwintered leafy greens will emerge and give you an early spring harvest; cut the whole plants in spring before they bolt.

EARLY WINTER PLANTING

No grow time: When daylight is less than 10 hours each day, plants in the garden will stop growing. If protected from cold they will not die, but they will not actively grow where there is less than 10 hours of sunlight; they will enter a period of dormancy. This is true for all plants including vegetables and herbs. The no-grow period can last two to three months depending on where you live (check the weather service for sunrise and sunset where you live). Leave crops in place and protect them from the cold; when daylight hours are again greater than 10 hours, vegetables will resume growth toward maturity and harvest. (Spring cabbage, for example, is planted in late summer or early autumn. It grows to near maturity but then stops growth and sits near dormant during the winter no-grow time; then in early spring as daylight increases the cabbage resumes growth, reaches maturity, and is harvested in spring.)

Garlic can be planted from autumn to early spring where the ground is workable. Garlic planted in autumn and early winter will be harvested the next mid-summer. Plant soft neck garlic if you live where winters are mild. Plant hard neck garlics where winters are cold and where springs are cool and wet. Be sure to plant garlic at least 4 to 6 weeks before the ground freezes; this will allow for the development of a strong root system. Garlic leaves can be chopped and used like chives.

Pixie tomatoes, *grow* pixie tomatoes indoors this winter in a pot in a sunny window or under grow lights. Pixies are very sweet, meaty, juicy, and flavorful—perfect for salads and garnishes. They are ready for harvest 55 days after transplanting.

Sow cress seed indoors. Grow cress indoors in a flat or shallow pot for sprouts. Fill the flat with seed-starter mix or organic potting soil, sprinkle the seeds across the soil, and then lightly cover the seed with seed-started mix or vermiculite. Seed will germinate in 2 to 6 days and be ready for harvest at 2 to 3 inches tall in two weeks. Cress has a peppery tang. Add cress to salads, sandwiches, and vegetables dishes.

Growing herbs indoors in *winter grow* culinary herbs in a sunny window for winter use. Annual herbs can be started from seed. Sow seed in 3- to 4-inch pots so they will have room to grow through the winter.

Chapter 5
Maintaining Your Vegetable Garden

Your vegetable garden is now planted and in the ground. So the hard work is done, right? Not quite. From now until harvest time, you need to maintain your garden so that your veggies are healthy and happy. When they are, they will reward you with a massive yield that will leave you harvesting a ton of delicious (and healthy) treats to add to your dinner table.

We'll start by covering fertilizers, which will build on the nutrient to provide your plants with the necessary building blocks for a large yield. Next, we will discuss how and when to water your veggies, which happens so often that you'll be an expert by the time of your first harvest. Then we will discuss how you go about weeding your vegetable garden to remove harmful intruders that want to eat up all the nutrients in the soil. Finally, we look at a bunch of micro-maintenance which will take no time at all to do but will keep your plants healthy and happy.

How to Fertilize Your Vegetable Garden

Fertilizer is an important piece of making sure that your vegetables grow healthy and strong. However, many people seem to think that fertilizer is some kind of magic potion for plants. This results in two misinformed ideas. Some people think that fertilizer fixes all problems; instead of identifying issues such as overwatering or poor temperature, these gardeners increase the strength of their fertilizer and expect their plants to start looking healthy suddenly. The other issue believes that more fertilizer is always a good thing. This is simply not true; it is the opposite that is true. Plants being overfed fertilizer may burn themselves by absorbing too many nutrients. Still, more often too much fertilizer messes with the pH level of the soil and makes it so the plants can't absorb any nutrients. To avoid these problems, you should always stick to the directions printed on the labels of whatever fertilizer you are using and you should educate yourself on fertilizers in general.

You could mix your fertilizer if you wanted to but this isn't recommended for beginners. It is better to purchase fertilizer that has already been formulated to meet your needs. Not only does this ensure that what you are using does what you want it to, but it will also provide you with directions on its use. Unfortunately, even purchasing a fertilizer can be a little confusing. As you're looking at bags or bottles of fertilizer you'll see a bunch of numbers that are different on each bag. This can be intimidating to some people because they instinctively think that it means they are going to have to do math but thankfully the reality is much simpler.

There are two ways to apply fertilizer. Most indoor or raised bed gardeners use a liquid fertilizer. This is made by purchasing either a liquid mixture that is diluted with water or a mixture of raw materials which is then dissolved in water. This is sprayed or poured onto the soil around the plants. However, many outdoor gardeners prefer to go with a solid fertilizer which is mixed into the soil itself. One way of doing this is to mix fertilizer in with the soil as you are making rows but before anything has been planted. When done in this way, the fertilizer is mixed to be spread out throughout the soil but under the top few feet so that the plants' roots can find it as they grow. Another way is to pour a line of fertilizer along the side of the row.

The best way to determine how often and how much fertilizer to give your plants is to follow the instructions on the package, many gardeners will start their plants off with a smaller dosage to see how they respond to it before mixing it stronger and stronger until it is at the level recommended on the package.

Watering Your Vegetable Garden

Watering the plants is another one of the images that pop into people's minds when they think about gardening. Everyone knows that plants need water, though it seems that not everybody realizes just how much. Hydrogen is one of the macronutrients which plants need to live but too much hydrogen causes root rot and leaves your plants sick.

Too little water also leaves them sick, though it is typically better to err on the side of too little than too much. One of the clear ways that plants tell us they need water is to start wilting. However, before you go watering them, you need to make sure that the reason they are wilting is the lack of water. If you notice your plants are wilting around noon, avoid watering them right away. This is the time of day when the sun is at its hottest and it may be the heat that is causing the wilt. Wait a couple hours and see if your plants bounce back as the temperature cools off. If they don't, then they probably do need watering. If they do bounce back, wilting was a part of the way that the plants withstand their environment. Midday wilting is the plant equivalent to people sweating a lot in the heat.

Temperature and shade are tightly connected. The hotter your local climate is, the more often your plants will need to be watered. This is because heat makes water evaporate and this dries out plants quicker than cold. Whether your plants are in shade, partial shade or full sun will directly affect their temperature. You might be in a climate that isn't overly warm but your plants getting full sun will still dry out water quicker than plants which are in shade. You need to be aware that fluctuations in temperature, such as heat waves or cold patches, also change the rate of evaporation.

It is also a good idea to water your plants after a short rainfall. This might seem counterintuitive, but it makes more sense when you consider the watering instructions you are about to learn. A short shower will allow water to get a little ways into the soil but the goal with watering is to make sure that the water is going deep into the soil. A light rain shower won't penetrate very far down, so adding some water to your beds afterwards will help to turn it into a proper watering.

Weeding Your Vegetable Garden

When it comes to maintenance, you've probably noticed that fertilizing and watering your garden isn't a lot of work. You only fertilize once a week and you only water about twice a week. It would be great if growing your delicious vegetables was this easy but the real hardship comes in weeding your garden.

Weeds are simply plants which spread naturally and don't belong in your garden. Weeds are notoriously fast growing plants and can very quickly take over a garden bed if left unchecked. They then steal energy from your plants by using the nutrients and water that would normally be used by your veggies. Large weeds or a mass of them are also able to block rays of light from breaking through to your plants. All and all, they want to leave your plants dead and take over the garden to call their own. If you are to have any chance of stopping them before they do this, you need to learn to identify them when they first arrive. Weeds are easy to tackle when they're in their earliest stages but if you don't catch them here then they can put up a long battle.

Anytime you spot a weed, hack it away with a tool. Many gardeners will grab a weed and give it a sharp tug to pull its roots out. However, those roots might be intermingled with the roots of your plant and cause it damage and this negates any positive that came from removing it in the first place. Cut off the top of the weed and leave the roots alone. This may kill the intruder but some weeds are particularly resilient and can go through several such beheadings before they finally kick the bucket. This can be a long, drawn-out process but going at it this way avoids the risk of damaging your plants. Plus, depending on your mindset, it can be either really peaceful or really fun to weed a garden. Of course, some people find it neither and only consider it to be an annoyance. It just depends on the attitude you approach it with.

Other Maintenance Tasks

While fertilizing, watering and weeding are the big three, there are still a few maintenance tasks which you are going to need to do if you want to keep your garden healthy. There are also a couple tasks that you'll have to do if you want to make sure that your harvest goes smoothly and the veggies themselves are high quality. None of these tasks will take you very long, and a few of them only need to be done once, maybe twice, per crop. But skipping out on these tasks is a bad idea as doing so needlessly puts your garden at risk.

Some of these tasks could arguably be considered pest control and disease prevention techniques, such as removing dead plant matter which could harbor both. You should be building your pest control behaviors into your general garden maintenance routine so that you are never caught unprepared by an unexpected infestation or infection.

Disinfect Your Tools After Use: This is a common sense maintenance task that you wouldn't believe how many gardeners ignore. The reason it is ignored is likely one of ignorance and a lack of knowledge. As has been stressed throughout this book, plants are living creatures. They not only have a living biology but they can communicate their needs to us in their visual language. You should disinfect all of your tools, including your shovels, rakes or hoes. Still, you especially need to disinfect shears or anything else that has come into contact with the plants themselves. Trimming a plant is essentially a form of surgery. Imagine going in for an operation and finding out the surgeon used a dirty scalpel to cut you open. You wouldn't be surprised at all when the wound got infected or you caught a new disease. Yet many gardeners leave their tools dirty and use them again and again, only to be surprised when their plants end up sick. Always disinfect your tools at the end of the day after using them.

Set *up* Shade: Although you may be growing plants that love direct sunlight, there may be moments when the heat is too much for them. When faced with a heat wave, these plants may get burned or damaged. You should be checking the weather not only every day but also the extended forecast. If there are spikes in the temperature, you may need to set up shade for your plants. This isn't done to reduce the amount of sun the plants are getting (though this is a result of it), but rather to bring the temperature of the plants down a few degrees. Full sun veggies are going to want that sun, but they can handle a couple days of shade better than they can handle being burnt to death.

Chapter 6
Garden Process

Starting a garden may sometimes require a little bit of effort as you loosen the soil while preparing the ground, but before you grab the spade and start digging, let us go through the first few steps to starting your vegetable garden:

Step One: Deciding What to Plant

Deciding what you would like to plant should generally be based on the vegetables you generally eat. It is always fun to grow a variety of vegetables that the family enjoys and sometimes even to grow one or two new items. It is best not to waste your time and effort while growing vegetables that will not be eaten as they will only crowd your garden and go rotten.

If you are planting vegetables and you plan on feeding them to your younger children or toddlers, be wary of what you choose to grow as some vegetables are difficult to digest, especially if you have little ones that suffer from abdominal related issues.

Here is a list of vegetables that are really children friendly. Often getting the children involved in the process of planting and growing makes them to be inclined to eat their vegetables when they have finally matured and prepared for the meals.

Babies

The following vegetables are suitable for children due to their ease in digestion and high nutritional values:

✓ Squash

✓ Pumpkin

✓ Sweet baby carrots

✓ Sweet Potato

✓ Carrots

NB: For babies and little children, it is advisable to avoid the following vegetables as they are prone to cause gas and worsen indigestion: peas, broccoli, cabbage, cauliflower, cucumber, and onions.

Little Children

✓ Potato

✓ Courgette

✓ Sweet Pea

✓ Cauliflower

✓ Green Beans

✓ Asparagus

Older Children

✓ Mushrooms

✓ Broccoli

✓ Spinach

✓ Aubergine

✓ Sweet Corn

Make a list of the vegetables that you are interested in planting, so that, while purchasing the seeds or seedlings you can refer to it. The list will assist you in making choices and avoiding seedlings and seeds of vegetables that aren't suitable for your family. Remember that the list you write is just a guideline for choices because as you will soon discover, what you want to plant and what you can plant are very different steps altogether.

Step Two: Questions to Ask When Purchasing Your Seeds

Once you have a clear idea of what you would like to plant, you can make your way to your nearest nursery or store. The best way to go about making sure you purchase the correct seeds for your vegetable garden is to take a copy of the "handy check-list" below with you. You will need to answer each question for each choice of vegetables that you plan to grow. Most of the information can be found on the back of the packet that the seeds are packaged in. The other option, especially when you are not sure, is to ask one of the assistants for advice.

Check-List:-

1. Is it possible to grow this vegetable in my region in the current season? (Answer 'Yes or No')

2. Must the seed be sown directly into the ground or into trays first?

3. What will the vegetables need to be grown in?

4. What sort of soil do my vegetables need?

5. How much sunlight exposure will my vegetables require?

6. How often should this vegetable be watered and provided with nutrients?

7. Does my garden meet the above vegetable requirements? (Answer 'Yes or No')

Let's have a look at all of these questions in detail

1. Is it possible to grow this vegetable in my region in the current season?

Certain vegetables can only be grown in certain seasons and in certain conditions. It is not worth it to plant vegetables in the wrong season or in a Frost Belt area where you will only be getting yourself into disappointments.

When purchasing your seeds, be sure to check that it can be sown in the season you are in or in the upcoming season. Also check whether the seeds or seedlings can grow in your region. More often than not a shop or nursery will only stock seeds suitable to the area, but be sure to confirm this as sometimes you may be in a suburb prone to frosting or dry heat and these conditions may not be suitable to your seeds.

Now let's have a look at your seasonal vegetables:-

Winter

✓ Onions

✓ Lettuce

✓ Tomatoes

✓ Basil

✓ Kale

✓ Parsnips

✓ Brussels Sprouts

✓ Broccoli

✓ Beans

✓ Beets

✓ Cabbage

✓ Cauliflower

✓ Garlic

Spring

✓ Broccoli

✓ Cabbage

✓ Lettuce

✓ Celery

✓ Onions

✓ Tomatoes

✓ Eggplant

✓ Peppers

✓ Squash

✓ Cucumbers

✓ Lettuce

✓ Peas

✓ Beets

✓ Radish

✓ Spinach

✓ Carrots

✓ Lettuce

✓ Leeks

✓ Beets

✓ Spinach

✓ Swiss Chard

✓ Radish

2. Must the seed be sown directly into the ground or trays first?

As a gardener you will always have the option to plant your seeds into seedling trays using pure and fertile soil that will ensure maximum potential for growth. At a later stage when the seeds have germinated and you have seedlings, you can then move them into an appropriate garden bed.

However, some seeds require this and should not be sown directly into the ground. There are multiple reasons for this method and unless you are going to meticulously plant each tiny seed the exact required distance apart, sowing vegetables directly into the ground will only bring more work to you at a later stage. Once your vegetables have germinated, they will need to be a certain distance apart from each other to provide room for grow. Growing your seeds in a seedling tray allows you to place these vegetables exactly where they need to be.

If you sow them direct you risk them not growing at all due to late frost and overcrowding. In any case, if they do grow at all, they will be all on top of each other and you will have to pull them all out and replant them anyway. In most cases, these seedlings are damaged in the process or they lose some roots and do not transplant very well.

You will need some effort to sow seeds into a tray first and then transfer them to the next medium. Don't lose hope due to these processes. Planting seeds indoors gives you a head start on the growing season as you can plant them up to 6 weeks before the season begins and then transplant them as the season starts.

Many gardeners believe that with experience and having spent a few seasons in the garden, you will come to know when the final frost will be over, you will also know the soil conditions and how to alter them accordingly. Furthermore, you will also be experienced enough to plant the seeds according to the required depth and spacing.

3. What will the vegetables need to be grown in?

Another essential aspect that you should consider is how your vegetables will need to grow to reap the most benefits. Some vegetables will need to be grown in pots, while other flourishes well in beds. Some will need to be supported as they grow upwards, and others will need lots of space as they creep across the bed. For the very fancy gardener, you may have the option of a tunnel or greenhouse to grow your vegetables in. Despite that, you will still need to know the logistics of your vegetable growth.

4. What sort of soil do your vegetablesneed?

Soil can be a tricky element to any gardener, as it needs to have just the right balance to provide the most ideal growing conditions for your vegetables. It is always a good idea to bring along a small sample of soil from your garden so that the assistant can see what you may need to add to it. Seedlings are usually grown in seedling trays with a seedling mix.

Some soils are very acidic and may not need much fertilizer. Other soils are hard and may need wood chippings and saw dust to create better drainage. You may even have soil that is much like the red clay. You will find that generally there are four main types of soil: clay, silt, sand, and loam.

Whichever category your soil fits into, you should be able to purchase the necessary additives from your local nursery. Generally soil is made up of different sized soil particles and small stones. It also includes a layer of humus as well as organic matters in different degrees of decomposition. The rest of your soil is just air and water.

It is a healthy balance of these elements that create the perfect conditions for growing. If your soil is too wet or it is a muddy soil type that dries in clods, then your seeds will struggle to grow and may not emerge at all. Soil needs a good drainage, and in case is doesn't, then the water will block off the air supply to the roots.

These properties of soil are necessary because too much of one or the other effects how your garden will grow. An ideal soil type should be comprised of the following characteristics:

✓ The soil is loose.

✓ It drains well.

✓ There are no weeds.

✓ It has been composted.

If your soil seems to be clay, it will drain but it may take quite a while. Very sandy soil will drain quickly and dry out. To make both soils ideal for planting, you can add your compost. Compost will loosen up clay soil and provide more resistance for sandy soils. Be wary when adding manure to improve your soil – some manure can be very acidic.

Making your compost is very easy and you can use many of the scraps from the kitchen, which are usually thrown away.

6. How often should this vegetable be watered and provided with nutrients?

When it comes to watering your garden, some vegetables will require a little more attention than the others. Feeding your vegetables means topping them up with nutrients appropriate to that plant.

If you under-water your plants then the roots will not grow deep and strong enough to enable them to gather more nutrients to grow. If you over-water them, then the soil will become clogged and the air will not be able to pass through. As you become more experienced, you will learn which vegetables require more water than others. Generally vegetables will need about 1 – 2 inches of water a week. Be sure to watch the weather, since your watering requirements will be weather dependent.

7. Does my garden meet the above vegetable requirements?

By now you should have an idea as to whether or not your chosen location is ideal for the vegetables that you would like to plant. You may have to reassess your list but consider these last few aspects too.

The area in which you would like to plant your vegetables needs to be away from children playground, people walking paths, and animals that could perhaps trod over the plants or break them. Be sure to make the appropriate adjustments, be it fencing or higher shelves/fences to ensure you are not disappointed.

Chapter 7
Tips and Tricks to Avoid Parasites

There are certain insects which are well-known for their ability to destroy gardens. Japanese and flea beetles, aphids, caterpillars, individual worms and grubs, and other creatures have the capability to annihilate the plants and vegetables in a garden utterly. So, you really do have to take extra steps to get rid of them once an infestation occurs.

There are quite a few unique tricks that can be used to help control the population of pests in an organic garden. An interesting aspect of some of these methods is they encourage harmony with nature itself. One such process entails strategically placing certain plants in such a way that the garden ceases to be a welcoming place for certain pests.

The process is known as companion planting, and entails adding plants to the garden which repel bugs. The obvious benefit to this process is that it reduces the need to use harmful pesticides. Companion planting is an effective biological method to control pests.

One plant that can be a very good addition to an organic garden is garlic bulbs. Folklore shows us that garlic wards off vampires. Well, it can also ward off a lot of insects that are just as parasitic to plants as vampires are to humans. There are quite a few creatures that garlic wards off in a garden. Slugs, caterpillars, snails, and certain spiders and worms are known to be repelled by garlic. Garlic, however, should not be planted near peas, sage, and some other plants, because they will stifle the growth of the garlic. You may wish to plant them four to six inches away from any plant that you have in the garden.

Marigolds may be more popular than garlic as plants which can keep insects away. There are quite a few harmful bugs that do not like to be near marigolds. Marigolds can outright kill the bad nematodes that can harm a garden. There are a host of other plants and flowers which can also work effectively in a vegetable garden as an insect repellent. Basil, sunflowers, chives, and many more offer effective stop gap measures against the presence of bugs in a garden. You may wish to do a little research to see which plants repel the insects you are most concerned about. As with sprays, you do have to be wary about scaring away the beneficial bugs you want to attract to your garden.

Other flowers commonly used for companion planting in vegetable gardens are nasturtium, petunias, alliums, tansy, yarrow, zinnia, lupine and geraniums. An added bonus to this method is the colorful beauty they'll add to your garden.

Most herbs make wonderful companion plants in your vegetable garden for warding off pests as well. Suggested ones are dill, lavender, hyssop, thyme, tarragon, borage, chamomile, sage, fennel, caraway, chervil, cilantro, lovage, oregano, parsley, peppermint, and rosemary. You'll have the advantage of having wonderful herbs to flavor your tasty dishes with. One caveat with some of these herbs, however, including the mint family, yarrow, and tansy, among others, can aggressively take over too much of your garden. Those you may want to plant in containers and then set the containers in your garden.

Another suggestion worth mentioning is to have a couple of bat houses and birdhouses scattered throughout your yard and garden area. They are also natural predators of insects.

Chapter 8
Aromatic Herbs for All Years

Rosemary

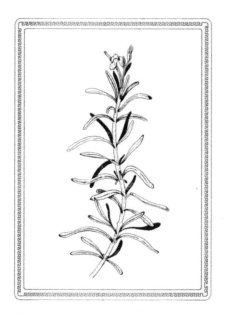

Widely used in the Mediterranean in cooking as well as a healing herb, Rosemary today has spread all around the world as it so easy to maintain both in a garden and in a pot.

This woody plant has countless benefits and not only as a wonderful and aromatic herb used with your meat dishes such as lamb.

Its scent will spread throughout your garden or on your balcony, and since it grows quite big (if you let it) it can turn into a natural fence that will keep curious eyes away as well as being used as an air fresher in the house.

It will smell amazing and freshens the house for days.

Rosemary's strong and slightly bitter taste can spice up the taste of your foods and beverages.

This plant is far more complicated and beneficial than you think and there is some research that it has anti-cancer properties.

Its tiny and pointy leaves grow on woody branches and do not lose their dark green color throughout the whole year.

Rosemary is not hard to grow and can be planted in almost every type of soil; it will even successfully grow in a rocky soil.

This is an ideal plant for people who truly don't want to spend a lot of time taking care of their plants and only needs a sunny place and watering every few days.

This is not one of those plants that crave moisture soils in order to grow, so do not flood it because you may damage the roots (the moist can cause rotting and the root itself can easily die from fungi).

Uses of Rosemary

This is excellent for skin irritations and joint problems like arthritis after it has been infused as oil.

It can help with the healing of wounds and bruises when used externally.

Basil

Basil is another well-known aromatic herb that comes from the mint family.

You may already know that basil as an aromatic and flavor-giving herb, but the basil is actually much more than a green décor with a fresh scent on the top of your pasta.

The plant has round leaves that are a little pointy.

Most often it is green but there are some varieties where basil can be red or purple.

To some extent Basil is a little like peppermint, but this is not surprising they both belong to the same family.

In fact, there are more than 60 varieties of this plant and they all have slightly different taste and appearance.

Benefits of Basil

Basil is packed with active constituents called flavonoids that are exceptionally important in the cellular protection and contains two water-soluble flavonoids Orientin and Vicenin.

Both play an important role not just in the role of cell protections but also in protecting the chromosomes from radiation and oxygen.

This gentle soft herb is also known for its power to protect the human's body from bacterial growth through its volatile oils that contain eugenol, myrcene, limonene, cineole, and linalool.

St. John's Wort

This wild yellow flower is also known as rosin rose or goat weed is not only widely spread across Europe, but also the Middle East, Asia, and the Americas.

It got its official name after St. John the Baptist, mostly because it is in full bloom by the end of June, for the saint's feast day (June 24)

It has always been used in different forms such as tea, oil, tincture; as well as in modern-day offering it in the form of capsules, creams, syrups and so on.

This plant is best known for its oil's miraculous effect but St. John's Wort has far bigger use than just that.

Anti-depressant, Relieves Anxiety

Perhaps not many people know that St. John's Wort has a very strong anti-depressant effect.

This plant has a very rare combination of antidepressant chemicals that prevent the reuptake of dopamine, serotonin, and norepinephrine, which leads to reducing the symptoms of depression.

Even today this is the first natural go-to remedy that psychiatrists prescribe to their patients.

People with anxiety are also encouraged to consume St. John's Wort mostly in the form of a tea.

Not only it soothes the anxiety but it also helps with mood swings. No wonder people used this herb to prepare tea in the long and cold winter months when depression and mood swings are more likely to happen.

Garlic

Garlic made its way to this list because it is a plant that has wide use in every kitchen in the world and because of its superpowers that can beat even the most persistent viruses and bacteria.

Even the Greek physician Hippocrates called garlic the father of Western medicine.

Garlic belongs to the Allium (onion) family and is 'relative' to onions, leek, and shallot.

This plant grows all around the world and is mostly known as a food ingredient because of its scent and taste.

There are historical proofs that garlic was used in the ancient Egyptian, Roman, Chinese, Greek, and Babylon.

Garlic contains one large 'head' while the little pieces that make the head are called cloves.

Most of its health effects come from the sulphur compounds that are released when the garlic is chewed or chopped.

Benefits of Garlic

The plant is rich in vitamin B6, Manganese, Selenium, Vitamin C, fiber, but it also contains lower amounts of vitamin B1, iron, potassium, copper, and phosphorus.

A Fighter *against* Colds and Flu

This is a famous fact and is 100% true for if consumed regularly it will boost the immune system.

Garlic is an antimicrobial, antifungal and antiviral plant that works like a miracle when comes to fighting the common colds and many infections.

The plant contains allicin which gives this vegetable its antimicrobial powers.

The great thing about this plant is that you can add it to any of your favorite dishes (soups, stews, meat, and pasta) or eat it raw.

Lowers the Risk of Cancer

People who consume raw garlic at least twice a week have lower chances of lung cancer than people who consume raw garlic less often or not at all.

These were the results of a seven-year study that was published in 2013 (Cancer Prevention Research).

This delicious plant is also quite beneficial for prevention and treatment of pancreatic or colon cancer.

Sage

Benefits of Sage

An Antiseptic

Sage is a natural antiseptic, which successfully kills bacteria in meat.

In the medicine, it is used for muscle aches, rheumatism, but also for aromatherapy (it smells heavenly).

Sage's oils contain ketones, including A- and B-thujone, that will improve memory and clear the mind.

This is why Sage is often used in treating cognitive decline and Alzheimer's.

Excellent for the Lungs, Heart, and Blood

Three-lobed Sage will provide you flavone saligenin that is a natural way to prevent yourself from cardiovascular disease.

Besides rich in flavonoids, phenolic acids, and the superoxide dismutase and peroxidase, Sage also contains antioxidant powers that will neutralize harmful free radicals.

This aromatic herb is great for fighting bronchial asthma, atherosclerosis, and inflammations.

Chapter 9
Advice for Growing Plants Fruit

If grown from seed, a strawberry plant takes up to three years before it will give you your first proper strawberry yield, but if you're not patient enough to wait, there is a way that you can plant a strawberry plant and have it producing strawberries within 12 months. This is made possible by using a cutting from an already-established strawberry plant, instead of trying to start one from seed. Strawberry plants that grow from cuttings are basically clones of the plant that the cutting was originally taken from, while strawberries grown from seed are genetic individuals. This means that by growing from cuttings, you can be more certain of the kind of plant you'll end up growing as well.

In order to take a cutting from a previously existing strawberry plant, you need to cut off about four inches (10 centimeters) from the existing plant's stem. You should then remove any shoots or leaves from this part of the stem. Once you've done this, these cuttings need to be dipped in a rooting hormone gel. You can buy this through online hydroponic stores, or at your local horticultural store. Of course, like nearly anything in this world, you can also make your own at home.

You can use a mixture of apple cider vinegar and water to create your own rooting hormone solution (three teaspoons to one gallon/four liters of water). Alternatively, you can also make a rooting hormone gel by using honey and boiling water. To do this, you should take one tablespoon of honey and mix it into two cups of boiling water, after which you should leave the mixture to cool before dipping your cuttings into it. If you don't have apple cider vinegar or honey on hand, you could use aspirin to make a rooting hormone solution too. In order to do this, you should take about a tablespoon of crushed aspirin and mix it into a gallon (four liters) of water.

If you're looking to cut costs, human saliva also makes a fantastic rooting medium. Dipping your cuttings in human saliva, or even licking them, should work nearly as well as a store-bought rooting hormone gel.

Once you've dipped your cuttings into a rooting hormone solution, you should then transfer them to your growing medium. They should start growing roots within a couple of days.

You should also make sure that the variety of strawberries that you are growing are day-neutral (like Hecker, Seascape, and Quinault strawberries), as these are the easiest to grow in a hydroponic system.

Strawberries yield the biggest possible harvest when grown at a pH level between 5.8 and 6.2, so be sure to check and adjust your reservoir's pH level regularly.

Your strawberry plants will need to be supplemented with at least potassium, nitrogen, and phosphorus in order to survive, but if you want to increase their yield significantly you should also supplement them with chlorine, cobalt, molybdenum, copper, manganese, zinc, and iron (so be sure to make or use a nutritional supplement containing these in order to get the best results).

Remember not to harvest your strawberries before they've turned blood red and are clearly ripe, as strawberries, unlike many other fruits, do not continue to ripen after being picked.

When it comes to blueberries, beginner hydroponic farmers should stick to varieties which are known to have a high success rate when grown hydroponically, namely:

- Top hat blueberries;

- Biloxi blueberries;

- Sunshine blue blueberries;

- Bluecrop blueberries;

- Powder blue blueberries;

- Brightwell blueberries;

- Pink popcorn blueberries;

- Legacy blueberries; and

- Pink icing blueberries.

Blueberries are one of the few popular hydroponic crops which thrive in an acidic environment. You should keep your hydroponic system's pH level between 3.5 and 5.5 when growing this crop. This means that blueberries should not be farmed in the same hydroponic system as other crops (unless, of course, the other crops share this preference for acidity, which is a rare occurrence). Your growing area should reach a maximum temperature of 74°F (23°C) and a minimum temperature of 68°F (20°C) in order to increase your blueberry crop's yield.

Make sure that the humidity in your grow room remains steady and doesn't suddenly increase or decrease, as fluctuations in humidity can increase the risk that your blueberry plants will develop anthracnose or gray mold. If you find that your blueberry plants are producing hard, inedible, tan-colored berries, it could be that your plants are suffering from mummy berry. Mummy berry is caused by a fungus called Monilinia vaccinii-corymbosi, and is caused by seed or cross-contamination. It's important that if you see any plants displaying signs of mummy berry that you remove them from your system and destroy them immediately in order to stop them from infecting their healthy counterparts.

Chapter 10
Problem Solving

Did You Choose a Good Garden Site?

What did you like about the site you picked? What would you change about it? If the site did not work well, evaluate different sites or different gardening methods. If you chose to grow in your backyard but found you preferred to grow in containers, maybe you can plan to use more containers next year. Were you satisfied with all of your vegetables? Would you like to grow different vegetables? More vegetables? Fewer vegetables?

There is always something new to learn about your garden site and growing vegetables. Take a course at your local community center, go on gardening tours, take a seminar, or join a gardening club. These are all fabulous ways to learn more and connect with fellow gardeners.

If you reinvented an old site or grew in an existing garden what worked and what did not? What would you need to do to make it even better next year? Gardening is always a work in progress. Plants grow and die back, some do better than others in your soil conditions, the weather and sunlight affect how plants grow, and unexpected problems always crop up. By taking the time to revisit your gardening season, you can write down ideas and plans for next season.

Did Your Plants Get Enough Sunlight and Rainfall?

Most vegetable plants need an average of six hours of sunlight a day and one inch of water every week to grow their best.

Did your site get the amount of sunlight you thought it would? If not, can you move your garden to another area? What other changes can you make? The sun shifts over the season, so what was in full sun in the spring may not have been in the summer and fall months. Do you need to plan your vegetable plantings to take advantage of this? If you know part of your garden is going to be in shade in the hot summer months, perhaps your lettuces will do better in a given spot than your tomatoes. Take time to re-examine your garden rotation.

Gardening can be a very creative pursuit. Designing and planning your vegetable garden layout each season can be a way to express your creativity. Use your creative or artistic abilities to create structures, sculptures, or use garden ornaments to make your garden special for you and your family.

Water, like sunlight, is essential for growing vegetables. Did you take into account the amount of rainfall you did or did not get? When you watered was it an easy or a difficult process? Do you need to make changes on how you watered your veggies? How you water certain vegetable plants can affect how they grow and what pests or diseases they may attract. Now is the time to make a list of any new hoses, water wands, or nozzles you have or may want to purchase for next season.

Did You Have Too Many or Too Few Vegetables?

Did you and your family eat what you grew? Did you plant too much or too little of any vegetables? Were you surprised about what grew really well or did poorly? Did the family like something you tried as an experiment? Jot down notes so you remember what you want to plant next season.

Growing healthy, safe food is a priority for some gardeners. Because there are more food scares and more product recalls, it is more important than ever to know where your food is grown. If you can grow your own vegetables and fruits, you will create a healthier life for yourself and your family.

Be careful not to mistake a bumper crop for overplanting. The perfect soil conditions and the perfect amount of water, sunlight, and heat can give you an overabundance of a certain vegetable. If you planted four cucumber plants and had too many for your use, think about scaling down to three plants. If you still have too many cucumbers the second season, perhaps you have the perfect garden for cucumbers! You can then scale back a bit more. However, remember that each year may bring different challenges, so plant at least two of everything to ensure you will have some veggies to eat.

Is there anything you can do to improve the growing conditions of the veggies that did not do so well? Not every vegetable will grow well in every site. Certain vegetables need more warmth, sunlight, or protection from the elements than others. Would certain plants do better in a container on your front patio than in the backyard? Do you need a greenhouse or cold frame to give your plants that extra warmth they need? If a vegetable plant consistently does not do well in your garden, try growing it in another way or acknowledge your site is just not what that plant needs. It does not mean anything about you as a gardener.

Did You Have Pest Problems?

It never fails. You finally feel you have vanquished the pests in your garden and something new shows up! No garden is pest-free—nor do you necessarily want it to be. There are beneficial and harmful insects and organisms and they both need to coexist for a healthy vegetable garden.

Gardening can be a very pleasurable experience. Having a vegetable or flower garden in your backyard, patio, or balcony can add beauty to your home. Plants can attract wildlife, birds, butterflies, and other insects that are beautiful to watch and enjoy. Take the time to really experience your garden.

What is important is to document your problem pests, what you did to prevent or get rid of them, and your results. This is valuable information to have for the seasons to come, although not every season will have the same problems. If something worked one season it will probably work again. If, however, something did not work, you do not want to waste your time doing the same thing again next season!

Tilling your garden beds is one way to expose any insects and larvae to the elements, which will make it harder for them to survive. Planting a cover crop or using mulch will keep your soil healthy. Keeping your plants healthier makes it easier for them to fight off any harmful pests. Once the garden is winding down in the fall, put up new fences or fixes the ones that were not working to keep out any unwanted animals.

Did You Have the Tools You Needed?

As a new gardener, good quality tools can be expensive. Buying a good tool every season may be the most economical way to get everything you want. Now that you have a growing season under your belt, you can make your list of what you need and a separate wish list. Proper tools for the job and the proper fit for the gardener can make vegetable gardening more fun and easier on the body.

The fall is a great time to make your list and catch some sales. It is also very important to take care of the tools you already have. Keeping tools clean all season long is a habit every gardener should have. Tools also need to be stored properly for the winter. If you do not have a garage or garden shed, find another protected area to store them—under a patio, under your front steps, attached to a wall that has an overhanging eave, or even under a large tree covered with a tarp to keep them somewhat protected from the weather.

What Do You Want to Try Next Season?

Imagine your perfect vegetable garden. What do you see in your perfect garden next season? What steps do you need to take to make it that way? Small and inexpensive changes can make a huge difference in how your garden looks and how well the vegetables grow. It is fun to experiment with planting vegetables that may not be common to your area or trying a new variety.

Trying something new can renew your interest if the garden is becoming a bit stale or your interest is waning. If you have a wild area and prefer a manicured garden, it may take some money and effort to make it happen, but it can be done. If you have recently moved into a new home and the garden is not quite to your taste, now is the time to make plans to change things. It may take several seasons, but it all starts with a dream and then a plan of action.

Was the Garden Too Large or Too Small?

Novice gardeners in particular find it challenging to assess the resources they need to plant, grow, maintain, and harvest a vegetable garden. How did you do? If you struggled to keep the area you had in reasonable shape, do not feel bad about scaling back a bit. If you started out small and feel you can easily go larger, then take the time to see how best to expand your garden site.

Weeds are often easy to control in a new garden site. When an area is newly tilled, weed seeds are often killed off. In other cases, the soil may not be as fertile, so the weeds do not grow as well. But beware. In the second or third season, weeds often seem to get out of control. Take that into consideration if you want to expand your garden. Once you start adding compost and amendments to your garden soil, both your veggies and your weeds will grow faster and bigger. If you can't decide whether to expand, try growing in the same-size area for a second season and then make your decision.

Chapter 11
FAQ

I have tried to give you a basic, but thorough beginner's guide to the most common and popular gardening methods. The emphasis has been on the mechanics of gardening. Now I want to bring it all together by answering the questions people tend to ask once they decide to try their hand at gardening. Some of the answers may be repetitions of things you have already read, but that is okay. If it is important enough to put in here twice, it's important enough to read it twice. So, without further ado...

Q: Is it better to start from seed or seedling plants?

A: Most of the times you will do better if you start your flowers with seedling plants. The main reason for this is that flowers take much longer to mature than vegetables. The exception to this is zinnias and sunflowers. You will also find that planting iris and lilies using just the chromes will work just fine, too.

When it comes to vegetables, however, it is almost always better to start from seed, with the exception of tomatoes, which need to be started indoors if you want to enjoy the fruits of your labor before the growing season is over.

Q: Is there anything to the old sayings about planting according to the signs of the moon and other such things?

A: Yes, most definitely! For example, a new moon pulls water up from the ground, which in turn, swells a seed and causes it to burst open (germinate). That is why planting within a day or two of the new moon causes quick productivity.

Q: What's the difference between garden soil and potting soil?

A: Potting soil is less dense. It contains little or no actual dirt/soil, but is a combination of peat moss, vermiculite or perlite, sand, and even finely ground tree bark. Potting soil has also undergone a sterilization process to kill any weeds and seeds that would interfere with plant growth. Garden soil contains actual soil, so it is much denser and doesn't drain as well as potting soil, and it tends to get packed down in pots.

Q: What about succulents? Are they easy to grow?

A: Yes. Succulents, which include cactus, are very easy to grow. They require next to no care and prefer not to be watered very often. In fact, I know people who have beautiful cacti that grow well with only a tiny bit of water every month or so. There are so many varieties of succulents to choose from, you can have a diverse and attractive display with very little work on your part. NOTE: Succulents do best in containers in most parts of the country.

Q: Are berries easy to grow, and can they be grown in small areas?

A: Strawberries are very easy to grow and can be grown in an area as small as 5x5 feet. Strawberry plants are a lot like bunnies—they multiply rapidly. You will need to thin your plants out each spring before they begin to bloom. You do this by simply pulling some of the plants out of the ground. You will also have to break their runners to separate them from their 'parent' plant. Sell or give your excess plants to someone. Blackberries, blueberries, raspberries, and all other berries require a lot more room and attention.

Q: Is one kind of mulch better than another?

A: Mulch is a matter of opinion. When you think of mulch, you tend to think in terms of cypress, cedar, or pine wood chunks. But there are actually several other materials you can use for mulch. They include rubber, pea gravel, creek gravel, nut hulls, cocoa bean hulls, and lava rock. Deciding what you use to mulch your gardens (if you use anything at all) depends on a number of things. For example, if your garden consists primarily of perennials, or if you have an area of your yard designated for pots, rock is often your best option. It doesn't have to be replaced, it doesn't attract insects (like wood does), and it requires next to no maintenance. Vegetable gardens or flower beds you will be tilling or spading every season don't need mulch. And finally, be sure your pets won't ingest the nut hulls, cocoa bean hulls, or rubber, as all are toxic to them.

Q: What are community gardens?

A: Community gardens are gardens used and tended to by several individuals. Most community gardens rent space to people to use for growing vegetables and herbs. Each person is responsible for keeping their own area of the garden weeded, watered, and tended to. I'll be honest—I don't know how community gardens keep people from taking things that aren't theirs. I assume it's based on an honor system, which should work. If you participate in a community garden venture, you still need to have your own tools, fertilizer, pest prevention, and so forth. Community gardens can be a great way to enjoy raising your own herbs and vegetables as long as you don't get tired of traveling back and forth to take care of your space.

Q: How do I know what planting zone I'm in?

A: This map shows the different planting zones in the United States.

Q: What flowers attract hummingbirds and butterflies?

A: Impatiens, petunias, hollyhocks, honeysuckle, bee balm, columbine, lilies, and phlox are a few of the most popular hummingbird attractants. Hibiscus, coneflowers, butterfly bush, sunflowers, lilac, zinnias, sweet William, petunias, and dianthus are just a few of the many flowers that will bring butterflies to your garden.

Q: Is it better to overwater or underwater your plants?

A: Neither. You need to make sure your plants get the amount of water they need AND that their home (ground, raised bed, or container) has proper drainage. When your plant is getting too much water, leaves will become pale and yellow and the plant will look limp. If they aren't getting enough water, leaves will drop in an effort to conserve food and energy for the main part of the plant.

Q: I see all sorts of unconventional things being used as flower or vegetable containers. What special preparation, if any, needs to be done to use these things?

A: Using 'unconventional' items to pot plants and flowers in is a great way to add a bit of whimsy and personal flair to your landscape. Flowers and plants look fine in traditional pots, but they look spectacular in an old suitcase, a cowboy boot, a vintage child's dump truck or lunch box, a dresser no longer in good enough condition to hold clothes, or whatever else appeals to you. The only preparation you need to make is to ensure the container has adequate drainage, so plants don't become waterlogged.

FYI: Other unusual items you can use for your container garden include:

- Old tins

- Purses

- Wheelbarrow

- Baskets

- Old tires

- Wooden boxes

Q: What things are compostable?

A: The most compostable materials are:

- Vegetable peelings

- Leaves

- Straw

- Sawdust

- Pine needles

- Small sticks

- Bark

- Paper towel and toilet paper tubes

- Newsprint (not glossy)

- Dryer lint

- Egg shells

- Coffee grounds

- Dead plants

- Stale bread, crackers, cereal

- Burlap

- Livestock manure

Q: What things can't I compost?

A: You cannot compost:

- Diseased plants

- Meat, pasta, bones

- Synthetics

- Walnut hull, leaves, and twigs

- Pet manure

- Human waste

- Plastic

- Glossy paper

- Dairy products

Q: How do I know if my soil is too acidic?

A: You can have a professional soil test done without spending a lot of money. You can also do it yourself using nothing more than a sealable clear glass jar, soil from your garden, and water. To test your soil, fill the jar about half full of soil from the garden you want to test. Fill the jar the rest of the way with water, leaving about an inch of space at the top. Seal the jar and shake it vigorously. Let it set untouched for 24 hours. During this time the soil will separate into layers of silt, clay, and sand.

You also need to notice the color or tint of your soil. The lighter the soil's color, the less organic matter it contains. If this is the case with your soil, you need to add compost matter to it to help your plants grow.

Chapter 12
What to do When Winter Grows Near

1: Winter/Autumn Vegetables

When we talk about growing winter vegetables, it has to be made clear that unless you live in warmer climes then we are really talking about planting in the early fall, and reaping the benefits as the early winter progresses.

Alternatively they can be planted in the late spring, usually a couple of weeks before the last frosts, to be ready for harvesting before the warmer weather arrives.

The bottom line is that once temperatures start to drop below 35F then even hardy cool season seeds will not germinate.

Once the plant has germinated and is growing however, then it is a case of protecting it from sudden drops in temperature – especially in the evenings.

The two main categories of vegetables in cool season we are talking about here are Hardy vegetables and semi-hardy vegetables.

All cool season crops taste better when they mature in the cooler weather, and are therefore best suited to planting in the late summer or early spring seasons.

Hardy Vegetables include - broccoli, cabbage, kohlrabi, onions, lettuce, leeks, peas, radish, spinach, turnips.

These veggies will grow in temperatures as low as 35-40F and will survive a light frost, especially if protected by a garden fleece covering..

It is not only the temperatures that restrict winter growth however, the shorter winter daylight hours mean that the plants may not get the minimum of 6 hours daylight required in most cases for garden vegetables.

The growing season of all vegetables and not just Hardy types can be extended considerably by the use of cold-frames, and polytunnels that will protect the plants against the worst of the winter weather.

Planting Times:

When planting seedlings or from seed itself, it is important to consider the time it takes for the plant to reach maturity, or at least to become harvestable. For instance planting too late in the Fall may mean that the plant will not reach maturity before the winter really closes in.

Planting beets or swedes too late in the springtime may mean that the hotter weather will cause the plants to bolt and become inedible.

With that in mind, here is a simple chart covering the growing times and required ground temperatures, for a selection of the most popular hardy vegetables you may consider for your winter veggies.

Another point to consider is whether or not you will be growing your vegetables under cover. As mentioned earlier, the use of a greenhouse, polytunnel, or cold-frame can mean that you are able to grow quite effectively in otherwise vegetable-intolerant conditions.

A polytunnel for instance that has perhaps been used to grow tomatoes during summer in cold northern regions, can be put to great use by growing a whole range of vegetables in cool season.

VEGETABLE	MINIMUM TEMP. F	OPTIMUM TEMP. F	APPROX. DAYS TO HARVEST
HARDY VEGETABLES			
BROCCOLI	40	80	65
CABBAGE	40	80	85
KOHLRABI	40	80	50
ONIONS (set)	35	80	65
LETTUCE (leaf)	35	70	60
LEEKS	40	80	120
PEAS	40	70	65
RADISH	40	80	30
SPINICH	40	70	40
TURNIP/SWEDE	40	80	50
SEMI-HARDY			
BEETS	40	80	60
CARROTS	40	80	70
CAULIFLOWER	40	80	65
PARSLEY	40	75	80
PARSNIPS	35	70	70
POTATOES	45	80	125
SWISS CHARD	40	85	60

Growing in Raised Beds is also an effective way to increase the growing season, as the Raised Bed tends to warm up quicker as it is lifted up from the cold ground temperatures of winter.

2: Protecting Winter Vegetables.

Keeping your winter vegetables protected from the worst of the weather, is a no-brainer – especially after you have gone to all the bother planting them in the first place!

As mentioned earlier, this is considerably easier if you are growing your winter vegetables inside a polytunnel, cold-frame, or otherwise under cover.

Even in a polytunnel however, if the temperature drops below freezing it is advisable to cover your veggies with a gardeners fleece to protect against frost damage.

1. For Parsnips and other root vegetables, providing the temperature does not fall below 23F (-5c) then they can effectively be left in the ground and covered over with a mulch of leaves or straw to a depth of around 6 inches.

This exposes any grubs and pests to the last of the frost and kills them. Alternatively, during this digging-over process you can include the leaf mulch into the soil, rather than removing it to add much-needed organic material.

Do not worry too much about snow conditions, as snow acts as an insulator in most cases – protecting the veggies below. However if you are in an area that has severe penetrating ground frost, then it is best to harvest your root vegetables and store in a root cellar.

Alternatively store them in a sand-filled box in a garage or frost-free outbuilding.

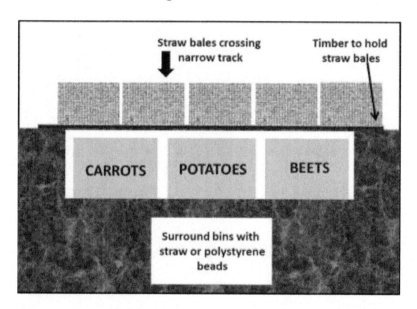

DIY ground-based root cellar

2. Garden fleece will protect your vegetables in cool season such as broccoli, salad crops, or winter cabbage against frost damage. Fleece or netting will also protect them from the ravages of pigeons!

Even an old blanket or hessian sacking thrown over the veggies at night, will protect them from the night-time drop in temperature – just remember to remove it again in the daytime.

3. Leeks can be lifted before the ground is frozen and 'heeled in' to a trench that is sheltered from the worst weather. They will last several months over winter in this situation.

4. Vermin can do a lot of damage to vegetable crops left in the ground over winter – especially if the weather is particularly bad and food is at a premium.

A couple of years ago I lost a good parsnip crop that had been growing in pots & containers to a family of rats!

They dug the parsnips right down the length of the root to get every last morsel – I was gutted, as was my wife who had been looking forward to honeyed parsnips for the Christmas dinner!

Needless to say the rats were promptly dealt with, however I had to buy the Christmas parsnips. Use whatever means at your disposal to deny them access, including ½ inch chicken mesh if need be, to be sure your roots are protected against mice and rats over the winter period.

Rats in particular are opportunists, and will nest near a food source if they can find one. Make sure there are no easy places for them to set up home such as piles of junk or other rubbish.

5. Build a cheap Polytunnel! This is not as hard as it might seem, and can be quickly achieved simply by bending plastic plumber's pipe into loops, and sticking the ends down into the soil.

Cover over with clear polythene, held down by soil along the length of the construction, and you have an instant – albeit a bit flimsy – polytunnel that will protect your plants admirably.

3: Planning Ahead

A truly successful gardener is one that is constantly planning ahead, not only for the next season, but also how to lay out the garden plot to get the best out of it, whether for vegetable production, flowers or just the aesthetics of the area.

Snowy cold winter days are an ideal time to relax by a good fire with a hot drink, and get your plans and schemes set out for the coming season.

Draw out a plan for your planting to be sure that the plants are properly rotated. This is essential to ensure you are not stripping out all the nutrients needed for the plants you plan to grow.

Consider companion planting requirements in order to restrict or even cut out entirely your need for chemical fertilizers or pesticides, whilst at the same time improving your crop yield.

Take note of areas where you may perhaps be planning a Raised Bed garden, and get to work sketching your ideas down or even constructing the frames themselves.

4: Misc Winter Tasks

Even if you are not actively gardening as such, there are numerous other tasks you can get involved in to prepared for the coming spring – and to stop boredom from setting in!

Pruning fruit trees and shrubs, although some do this over the winter period, I would advise against this practice mainly if you are in an area prone to hard frosts.

If this is the case then pruning can result in frost-damage to the newly pruned part of the tree. Far better to prune trees and shrubs in late Autumn or Spring, after the last of the winter frosts.

Transplanting of fruit trees can certainly be done over the milder winter period, preferably late Autumn. This will give time for the roots to be established for the spring growth.

Winter digging-in in order to expose the open ground (and the bugs) to the winter elements is something that is still widely practiced.

However if you are on sloping ground it is not advised so much, as it means that the nutrients in the soil are free to run-off after heavy rain or snow melt.

In this instance it is better to wait until just before the last frosts of winter before digging over and preparing for the spring planting.

Digging-in well-rotted compost or manure at this time will prepare the ground well for the spring growing or flowers or vegetable crops.

Ponds should have an area kept clear of ice by placing a football or some other floating object in whilst it remains unfrozen.

Removing this later will create a clear area for aquatics such as fish and over-wintering frogs and toads to breathe. Do not smash the ice with a heavy hammer if you can avoid this as it is likely to concuss and kill fish in particular.

Fill the bird feeders! Keeping your local bird-life well fed will help ensure their survival over a bleak winter, and help persuade them to stay around for the spring. This will ensure you have a healthy bird population to help you out with keeping destructive insects at bay.

Garden hoses should be drained before being neatly rolled and stacked away for the winter. Leaving the sprinklers or other fittings attached at the end of the hose is a bad mistake, as they will likely freeze and burst if there is still water in them.

Make sure you have adequate lagging on outside taps and pipes to prevent freezing. The outside tap water supply should be turned off and the taps themselves left open to prevent ice forming and splitting the fittings.

Fences and sheds that need to be repaired is a cold but essential part of the winter tasks to be done. Best however before the cold weather really closes in, as frozen fingers do not hold nails so well!

Composting, time to turn over the composting heap, add new materials and generally see to it that the composting bins are in good shape

If you do not already have one, then an excellent composting bin arrangement will pay dividends for years for very little expense. Here is an example of a triple bin composter made from old pallets.

This way, as the composting material in the middle bin rots down to a good level you can transfer it to the left hand bin. This means that with proper management you can have excellent composting material on hand on a near-constant basis.

Make sure that you position your polytunnel where it will get the best protection from the elements, as well as the most direct sunlight.

Chapter 13 10 Recipes Ready in 30 Minutes with Vegetable

Easy Vegetarian Wok Stir-Fry

This Asian-style stir-fried vegetable is packed with goodness in every bite.

Preparation Time: 10 minutes

Total Time: 20 minutes

Servings: 4 servings

Ingredients:

2 Tbsp. peanut oil

1 large red onion, sliced

½ teaspoon garlic, crushed

2 cups broccoli, cut into florets

1 cup snow peas or snap peas, trimmed

1 cup green beans, cut into 2-inch pieces

1 medium yellow bell pepper, cut into strips

1 medium carrot, cut into thin strips

¼ cup vegetable stock or chicken stock

2 tablespoons soy sauce

1 teaspoon sesame oil

salt and freshly ground black pepper

Directions:

Heat oil; stir-fry the onion and garlic for 1 minute.

Add broccoli, snap peas, green beans, bell pepper, carrot, stock, and soy sauce. Cook for about 7-8 minutes until tender but still crisp, stirring frequently, season with salt and pepper. Stir in sesame oil. Remove from heat.

Transfer to a serving platter.

Serve and enjoy.

Nutrition: Calories: 400 Net Carbs: 5.9 g Total Fat: 39 g Saturated Fat: 22.3 g

Sautéed Cabbage Mushroom and Pepper

This sautéed vegetable recipe made with cabbage, mushrooms, and pepper is not only delicious but nutritious too!

Preparation Time: 10 minutes

Total Time: 25 minutes

Servings: 4 servings

Ingredients

2 tablespoons peanut oil

2 shallots, sliced

1 teaspoon garlic, minced

1 medium head cabbage, shredded

1 cup button mushrooms, sliced

1 medium red bell pepper, cut into strips

2 tablespoons rice vinegar

2 tablespoons soy sauce

salt and freshly ground black pepper

Directions:

Heat oil in a wok over medium-high heat, sauté shallots and garlic for 1 minute

Add the cabbage, mushrooms, red bell pepper, and cilantro. Cook for about 5-7 minutes, stirring frequently.

Stir in rice vinegar and soy sauce, cook further 2 minutes, season with salt and pepper. Remove from heat.

Transfer to a serving dish.

Serve and enjoy.

Nutrition:

Calories: 355

Net Carbs: 5.8 g

Total Fat: 42 g

Saturated Fat: 27 g

Herbed Garlic Mushroom Stir-Fry

This simple Vegetarian-friendly recipe only calls for 5 necessary ingredients.

Preparation Time: 5 minutes

Total Time: 15 minutes

Servings: 4 servings

Ingredients:

1 tablespoon butter

1 teaspoon olive oil

1 teaspoon garlic, minced

2 cups button mushrooms, whole

¼ cup fresh parsley, chopped

Directions:

In a large skillet or non-stick pan, heat butter and oil over medium heat. Stir-fry garlic until aromatic.

Add button mushrooms and parsley. Cook, stirring for 5-7 minutes.

Transfer to a serving dish.

Serve and enjoy.

Nutrition:

Calories: 256

Net Carbs: 5.0 g

Total Fat: 43 g

Saturated Fat: 12.3 g

Stir-Fried Mixed Vegetable with Beef Strips

This quick stir-fry made with mixed veggies and beef strips is really delicious.

Preparation Time: 10 minutes

Total Time: 20 minutes

Servings: 6 servings

Ingredients:

2 Tbsp. vegetable oil

1 medium onion, sliced thin

1 teaspoon garlic, minced

1 pound sirloin beef, cut into thin strips

1 cup button mushrooms, sliced thinly

1 small head broccoli, cut into small florets

1 medium yellow bell pepper (capsicum), cut into strips

1 medium carrot, cut into thin strips

2 Tbsp. oyster sauce

2 Tbsp. rice vinegar

salt and freshly ground black pepper to taste

Directions:

In a large skillet or wok, heat oil. Stir-fry onion and garlic for 1 minute.

Add beef strips and cook for 3-5 minutes until browned, stirring frequently.

Add broccoli, mushrooms, bell pepper, carrot, oyster sauce, and vinegar. Cover and cook further 5-7 minutes, stirring occasionally, season with salt and pepper, to taste.

Nutrition:

Calories: 349

Net Carbs: 6.9 g

Total Fat: 32 g

Saturated Fat: 12.3 g

Chinese-Style Vegetable Stir-Fry

This simple dish is ideal for busy weeknights, so colorful and flavorful!

Preparation Time: 10 minutes

Total Time: 20 minutes

Servings: 4 servings

Ingredients:

2 tablespoons peanut oil

2 shallots, sliced thinly

2 cloves garlic, minced

2 cups broccoli, cut into small florets

1 cup baby corn or young corn, halved

1 cup snap peas, trimmed

1 medium red bell pepper, cut into strips

2 tablespoons light soy sauce

1 teaspoon Worcestershire sauce

salt and freshly ground black pepper to taste

Directions:

In a large skillet or wok, heat peanut oil over medium heat. Stir-fry shallots and garlic for 1 minute or until aromatic.

Add the broccoli, baby corn, snap peas, and red bell pepper, cook, stirring frequently for 5 minutes.

Stir in soy sauce and Worcestershire sauce. Cover and cook further 3-5 minutes, stirring occasionally, season with salt and pepper, to taste.

Transfer in a serving dish.

Serve and enjoy.
Nutrition:

Calories: 337

Net Carbs: 5.4 g

Total Fat: 34 g

Saturated Fat: 32.3 g

Sesame Vegetable and Shrimp Stir-Fry

This tasty and healthy vegetable stir-fry with shrimp and sesame seeds is a dish that you can easily prepare during busy weeknights.

Preparation Time: 10 minutes

Total Time: 20 minutes

Servings: 4 servings

Ingredients:

2 Tbsp. peanut oil, divided

8 oz. shrimps, peeled and deveined

1 medium onion, sliced thin

3 cloves garlic, minced

1 medium head broccoli, cut into small florets

1 medium red bell pepper, cut into strips

2 cups snap peas, trimmed

2 tablespoons light soy sauce

1 teaspoon Worcestershire sauce

salt and freshly ground black pepper to taste

toasted sesame seeds, to serve

Directions:

In a large frying pan or skillet, heat 1 tablespoon heat oil. Cook the shrimps for 2-3 minutes, stirring frequently. Transfer to a plate.

Using the same skillet, heat oil, stir-fry onion and garlic until fragrant

Add broccoli, bell pepper, and snap peas. Cook for 5-7 minutes, stirring occasionally. Stir in soy sauce and Worcestershire sauce. Season with salt and pepper.

Transfer in a serving dish. Sprinkle with toasted sesame seeds.

Nutrition:

Calories: 150 Net Carbs: 5.4 g Total Fat: 28 g

Saturated Fat: 21.3 g

Stir-Fried Bitter Melon with Egg and Tomato

This vegetable dish is popular in Asia, bitter melon is packed with nutrients like iron that is good for the health.

Preparation Time: 10 minutes

Total Time: 20 minutes

Servings: 4 servings

Ingredients:

2 Tbsp. olive oil, divided 1 medium onion, thinly sliced

½ teaspoon garlic, minced

2 medium tomatoes, sliced

1 medium bitter melon

1 medium carrot, cut into thin strips

2 large eggs, beaten

salt and freshly ground black pepper

Directions:

Cut both ends of bitter melon then slice in half (lengthwise). Scoop out the seeds and white pith using a spoon. Slice thinly crosswise or diagonally, about 1/4-inch thick.

In a medium saucepan, bring water to a boil. Add bitter melon and cook for 2-3 minutes. Remove from heat. Let sit for another 3 minutes. Drain. (This will help reduce the bitter taste)

Heat oil in a non-stick pan or skillet over medium-high heat. Stir-fry onion and garlic for 1 minute or until fragrant

Add the tomatoes, bitter melon, and carrot. Cook for 7-8 minutes, stirring frequently.

Add the beaten egg. Cook further 3 minutes, stirring constantly. Season with salt and pepper. Remove from heat. Transfer to a serving dish

Nutrition: Calories: 250 Net Carbs: 5.7 g

Total Fat: 25 g Saturated Fat: 21.3 g

Cauliflower Broccoli and Cheese Casserole

This vegetable casserole recipe made with cauliflower, broccoli, herbs, and cheese is so delicious!

Preparation Time: 10 minutes

Total Time: 30 minutes

Servings: 8 servings

Ingredients:

1 head broccoli, cut into small florets

1 head cauliflower, cut into small florets

1 medium onion, diced

1 (10.75 ounce) can condensed cream of mushroom soup

1 cup light mayonnaise

2 Tbsp. Dijon mustard

½ tsp. dried tarragon

½ tsp. dried sage

1 teaspoon garlic powder

½ cup bread crumbs

½ cup cheddar cheese, grated

¼ cup mozzarella cheese, grated

Directions:

Preheat oven to 350 F.

In a large bowl, mix together cream of mushroom soup, mayonnaise, Dijon mustard, tarragon, sage, garlic powder, and bread crumbs.

Add the broccoli, cauliflower, and onion. Mix well.

Transfer mixture to a baking dish. Sprinkle with cheddar and mozzarella. Bake for 20 minutes. Cool slightly.

Nutrition:

Calories: 388 Net Carbs: 6.9 g

Total Fat: 25 g Saturated Fat: 23.3 g

Easy Homemade Tabbouleh Salad

This Levantine-inspired recipe is viral in many parts of the world because of its unique taste and aroma!

Preparation: 15 minutes

Total Time: 15 minutes

Servings: 6 servings

Ingredients:

1 ½ cup cooked bulgur wheat

1 cup cucumber, diced

1 cup tomatoes, diced

1 cup flat-leaf parsley, chopped

1 cup mint leaves, chopped

1 cup green onion, chopped

salt and freshly ground black pepper

Lime Vinaigrette Dressing:

1/3 cup extra-virgin olive oil

1/4 cup lime juice

1 Tbsp. honey

salt and freshly ground black pepper

Directions:

Whisk together olive oil, lime juice, and honey in a small glass bowl.

Combine the bulgur, cucumber, tomatoes, parsley, mint, and green onions in a large salad bowl. Drizzle with vinaigrette. Toss to combine. Season with salt and pepper, to taste.

Nutrition:

Calories: 123

Net Carbs: 5.4 g

Total Fat: 33 g

Saturated Fat: 24.3 g

Fresh Caprese Salad

This 5-ingredient Mediterranean salad recipe is can be made in a snap!

Preparation Time: 10 minutes

Total Time: 10 minutes

Servings: 5 servings

Ingredients:

1 pound cherry tomatoes, halved

8 oz. fresh mozzarella balls

2 cups fresh sweet basil

salt and freshly ground black pepper

Balsamic Vinaigrette:

1/4 cup olive oil

2 Tbsp. balsamic vinegar

2 tsp. honey

Directions:

In a small bowl, whisk together olive oil, balsamic vinegar, and honey.

In a large bowl, combine cherry tomatoes, mozzarella and basil. Drizzle with prepared balsamic vinaigrette. Season with salt and pepper. Toss to coat.

Nutrition:

Calories: 433

Net Carbs: 5.7 g

Total Fat: 35 g

Saturated Fat: 25.3 g

Chapter 14 Other Things to Consider in Vegetable Gardening

Where Should You Put Your Garden?

The first decision you need to make is where to place your garden. Because it's challenging to change the location of your garden once you've built it, you should consider the following factors carefully.

Follow the Sun

Many of the most popular vegetables in home gardens require full sun. "Full sun" means a minimum of six to eight hours of unshaded, unfiltered sunlight during the growing season. Even though some vegetables and herbs tolerate less sunlight, it's best to choose the sunniest location possible for your garden.

Note that the angle of the sun's track changes throughout the year, so the sunniest spot in the off-season won't be the same as during the growing season. Consider where the sun will track in the height of summer. Also, keep in mind that a location near a deciduous tree may receive full sun in the winter but will remain mostly shaded in the summer when the leaves return.

Notice where a potential garden space would lie in relation to structures such as your home or a shed, in all but the hottest climates, gardens facing west and south will benefit the most from ample afternoon sun.

Site It within Sight

"Out of sight, out of mind." It may not seem like it now, but in the middle of the growing season, gardens not within easy walking distance of the house suffer more neglect than gardens located close by.

There is a saying that "the best fertilizer is a gardener's shadow." Daily walks in the garden allow you to spot and treat small issues before they become big problems. Catching problems early will lead to a healthier, more successful garden.

Access to Water (But Not Too Much)

If possible, try to position your garden near a water source such as an outdoor spigot. Easy access to supplemental irrigation will help you stay on top of the watering needs of your plants.

However, too much water can be a bad thing. Avoid placing your garden near rain gutters or in low-lying areas. I unknowingly situated my first garden, an entirely in-ground garden, in the lowest area of my property. Winter and spring rains puddled, and few plants survived. Take note of natural slopes in your land, and avoid placing your garden in the lowest-lying areas.

What Type of Garden Should You Have?

Raised Bed or Container?

Most raised garden beds have no solid base and therefore are open to the ground, allowing plant roots access to the soil below, whereas a container plant grows in a confined space.

Raised beds require simple construction, whereas containers can easily be purchased ready to go. Both types need to be filled with soil, but if you have access to native ground soil, you can use a mixture of that in a raised bed, saving money on soil costs.

Containers demand more frequent watering, which is a consideration if you're often away from home. Raised beds allow more viable options, but typically container gardens require less maintenance and labor overall.

Figuring Out Size and Shape

Most gardeners who can give an hour per week to garden tasks during peak season can easily manage a few raised beds. Although raised beds come in a variety of shapes and sizes, I recommend sticking with a conventional size. A simple 4-by-8-foot, 4-by-12-foot, or 3-by-6-foot bed provides plenty of plant layout options.

If you choose container gardening, you will likely find your limits not in the amount of time you can give but rather in your budget. Purchasing containers and soil can become costly. You can always start with a few containers and add more as your budget allows.

What Should You Grow?

Besides growing what you enjoy eating, other factors such as where you live and the gardening method you've chosen will also help determine what you grow. Let's take a look at these considerations.

Determine Your Growing Zone

Knowing your growing zone will help you understand your general growing climate and which plants will likely thrive there. Divided into 11 categories, growing zones are calculated based on the average annual minimum temperature in each location. (See the map to find your zone.)

Growing zones were created to help gardeners understand which perennial plants will survive the winter in a particular location. Because annual plants complete their life cycle in one season and do not survive the winter, growing zones technically do not apply to them.

Although your zone won't matter for most vegetables and herbs you grow, knowing it can help you understand which plants grow best in certain seasons, which plant varieties may grow better, and which plants may not grow at all.

Consider Your Garden Type and Space

Most plants are happy to grow in containers, raised beds, or the ground. However, some are better suited to one form or another.

Some herbs (e.g., mint, lemon balm, and oregano) spread aggressively, which makes them ideal for a container. If you plant them in a raised or in-ground bed, they will take over and smother other plants.

Some crops are considered "heavy feeders," which means they need more nutrients than others. Therefore, although heavy feeders such as tomatoes, squash, cabbage, and broccoli grow well in containers, they enjoy the moisture-holding capacity of raised beds, and the greater access to soil nutrients reduces the need for regular supplemental fertilizer. Raised beds are also ideal for crops that require more plants for a plentiful harvest, such as beans, peas, and okra.

Some plants also need more space than others. If you're looking to maximize the yield of your garden, a container full of greens that can feed you for months may be a better choice than a container with one cabbage plant that will give you one head.

Pick Plants That Get Along

Vegetables and herbs benefit from companion planting. Scientific research on the topic remains scarce, but we do know that the more diverse your vegetables, herbs, and flowers are, the healthier your garden will be. Some plants do seem to offer a measure of pest control to nearby plants. For example, icicle radishes may repel squash bugs and cucumber beetles.

Conversely, some plants negatively affect others when planted in close proximity, broccoli and tomatoes, for example, both uptake high levels of calcium. Planting them together could result in smaller broccoli heads and blossom-end rot in tomatoes. Also beware that plants in the same families (e.g., cabbage and cauliflower) often are visited by the same pests, are afflicted by the same diseases, and take up similar nutrients from the soil.

When and How Should You Plant Your Vegetables?

You're going to discover how to plan the timing of your plantings, start seeds indoors, plant directly in the garden, properly space your vegetables, and plan for crop rotation.

Figure Out Your Frost Date

Perhaps even more critical than your garden zone, your average last- and first-frost dates are crucial to your planting decisions.

In the spring, you plant each crop a specified number of weeks before or after your average last-frost date, depending on the plant. The same goes for crops you plant for a fall harvest, relative to your average first-frost date in the fall..

Starting Seeds vs. Sowing Directly

Many first-time gardeners choose to plant only transplants from the local nursery or garden center. But for others, the idea of planting seeds excites them, not to mention that many plants (beans, for example) do not transplant well and are best planted from seed. In addition, seeds are comparatively inexpensive.

If you do choose to plant seeds, you need to decide whether to start seeds indoors or direct sow them into the garden..

Other plants are best suited for direct sowing. Beans, squash, zucchini, peas, corn, carrots, spinach, and beets prefer being grown from seeds planted directly in the garden. Soil temperature is vital for proper germination, and I strongly recommend purchasing an inexpensive soil thermometer to ensure the soil is warm enough for sowing.

Each plant you plan to grow will require different planting times and soil temperatures; refer to the plant profiles in part 2 for specifics. If you're pressed for time and want to ease into your first garden, feel free to skip starting your seeds indoors. Many beginning gardeners purchase young plants and transplant them. In addition, some vegetable seeds germinate and grow better when planted directly into the ground.

Spacing

How do you figure out how far apart to space seeds or transplants?

Proper spacing is essential. If vegetables grow too close together, they compete for nutrients and water, reducing total yield. On the other hand, if they grow too far apart, weeds fill the vacant space.

Seed packets, plant tags, and the plant profiles in part 2 will give you direction on proper plant spacing. Seed packets generally direct you to "overseed," which means planting more seeds than will ultimately grow. After the seeds germinate, you remove extra seedlings by cutting them at soil level, in order to arrive at the final spacing.

Bear in mind that the recommended spacing on seed packets refers to rows of plants in a traditional in-ground garden. There are no pathways in containers and raised beds, so you won't need to leave as much room between rows. Instead, use the plant spacing recommendations for seeding, and plant in all directions. For example, you may be advised to plant bush bean seeds 3 inches apart in rows 2 feet apart, thinning after germination to a final spacing of 6 inches apart. In a raised bed or container, you can plant the seeds 3 inches apart in all directions, then thin to half the number of beans planted.

Succession Planting

You can get twice the harvest from the same space by succession planting, which means planting a second crop after production ends from a first crop. An example of this is planting summer squash after you harvest and pull up bush beans.

Relay planting offers even more options. In relay planting, you plant a second crop next to a crop that is nearing its end of production. The two crops grow side by side until the first crop comes out. I use relay planting when I place bell pepper seedlings between mature spinach or lettuce plants. As the summer heats up, these cool-weather leafy plants bolt. I pull them up and the bell peppers take over.

To get the most out of succession planting, it helps to know whether a crop harvests all at once, all season long, or until heat or cold stops its production. Root crops harvest all at once and fall into the "one harvest" category, whereas bush beans and peas harvest over only a couple of weeks and fall into the "quick burst" category. Pole beans provide an "all season" harvest, producing until frost, and many greens are "weather dependent," meaning they keep producing until heat makes them bolt.

Crop Rotation

When you consider all the possible combinations of plant locations and then factor in having to rotate your crops from year to year, you may find your head spinning!

Thankfully, crop rotation isn't terribly complicated. Follow this basic formula: Avoid planting vegetables from the same plant family in the same place season after season. The reason for this is twofold. First, some diseases and pests that plague one family of plants persist in the soil. By rotating susceptible crops out of that area, you disrupt the disease and pest cycle. Second, different crops absorb different amounts of nutrients, and some actually contribute nutrients to the soil. For example, corn and squash require large amounts of nitrogen relative to other crops, so changing their location each season prevents depletion of the soil and stunted plants. Beans, on the other hand, add nitrogen to the soil, so your garden will benefit if you change their position each season so they can spread their love.

Conclusion

Thank you for making it to the end. I hope that this book has helped you on learning the understanding the basics of Vegetable Gardening. As the world continues to embrace green living and sustainability practices, the number of people growing their own vegetables will keep rising. This interest is set to help the world in a lot of ways, such as by reducing the demand for chemically processed foods that ruin the environment. Another consequence of this movement will be a rise in clubs and friendships that are formed around gardening. Both of these are positive changes that you are helping to bring into the world by starting your vegetable garden. Since our gardens are outside, in the ground, seeding refers to the act of sowing seeds directly into garden beds where they will be raised through to harvest.

While this is the most common way for large-scale farming operations to start their crops, it is actually more often looked down upon by smaller scale gardeners. This is due to the fact that there is a higher risk of failure when seeding directly. While this added risk isn't overly much, it is enough to push many gardeners towards planting seedlings in beds instead.

Planting seedlings is achieved by first germinating seeds in small containers and allowing the seedlings that sprout up to grow strong enough to be transplanted to the garden bed. While this creates an extra step and is far more time-consuming, it allows the gardener to take a more active role in the growth of their plants. Thus, the rate of successfully starting a crop is increased. However, starting seeds in containers requires more attention, time, and resources, which can make it less attractive to some gardeners

Starting anything new is an intimidating experience for most people. As much as we enjoy surprises and trying new things, it takes effort to overcome the knowledge barrier that is needed to begin. If you just take a shovel out to your backyard and drop some seeds, you aren't going to have a very healthy garden. But by reading this manuscript you have already proved to yourself that you are willing to seek out the knowledge you need to get gardening properly. Where other beginner's jump in too soon, you have taken the time to understand the topic and the task at hand and this is the most beneficial thing you could do for the sake of the living organisms which you are growing to provide your family with dinner.

By this point you understand the importance of planning your own vegetable garden and that it isn't just about what you want to grow but also about where you grow it and how much care you are able to provide for it realistically. You know that the soil needs to be right, that there is such a thing as too much or too little sun, and that too much water is actually a very dangerous thing. You know the importance of fertilizing your plants but also its limitations, plus what it means to be NPK balanced.

Remember that raising healthy vegetables is first and foremost about looking after your plants, tending to their needs and maintaining their beds. Because of this you know how to protect them from pests and how to identify when they are ready to be harvested for the biggest and tastiest yield.

Printed in Great Britain
by Amazon

50996053R00088